Karl Marx, Friedrich Engels, Jenny Marx Longuet, Eleanor Marx Aveling, and Laura Marx Lafargue. Source: *Wikimedia Commons*

Eleanor Marx Aveling. Source: *Internet Archive*

# Jenny, Eleanor, and Laura, et al.

## This Is Not a Book About Marx

Valérie Lefebvre-Faucher

Translated by Mélissa Bull

Between the Lines
Toronto

First published in French by les Éditions du remue-ménage as Promenade sur Marx. Du côté des héroïnes, © Valérie Lefebvre-Faucher et les Éditions du remue-ménage, 2020.

This edition published in 2025 by
Between the Lines
401 Richmond Street West, Studio 281
Toronto, Ontario · M5V 3A8 · Canada
1-800-718-7201 · www.btlbooks.com



Library and Archives Canada Cataloguing in Publication
Title: Jenny, Eleanor, and Laura, et al. : this is not a book about Marx / Valérie Lefebvre-Faucher ; translated by Mélissa Bull.
Other titles: Promenade sur Marx. English
Names: Lefebvre-Faucher, Valérie, 1979- author | Bull, Melissa, 1977- translator
Series: Provocations (Toronto, Ont.)
Description: Series statement: Provocations | Translation of: Promenade sur Marx : du côté des héroïnes. | Includes bibliographical references. | In English, translated from the French.
Identifiers: Canadiana (print) 20240516265 | Canadiana (ebook) 2024051629X | ISBN 9781771136716 (softcover) | ISBN 9781771136723 (EPUB)
Subjects: LCSH: Women and socialism. | LCSH: Socialism—History. | LCSH: Communism—History. | LCSH: Marx, Karl, 1818-1883—Family.
Classification: LCC HX546 .L4413 2025 | DDC 335.4082—dc23

Cover and text design by DEEVE

Printed in Canada

We acknowledge for their financial support of our publishing activities: the Government of Canada; the Canada Council for the Arts; and the Government of Ontario through the Ontario Arts Council, the Ontario Book Publishers Tax Credit program, and Ontario Creates. We acknowledge SODEC for their financial support of the translation of this book. La traduction de cette œuvre a été rendue possible grâce au soutien financier de la Société de développement des entreprises culturelles (SODEC).

*For my friends*

# Contents

# Prologue

> To write is to walk until the point of departure is forgotten.
>
> —Louky Bersianik

This research reveals who I am as much as it does the Marxes. You can see me winding through a labyrinth of letters, picking paths out of curiosity. I'm a weird wanderer, amazed at finding paper trails between individuals from era to era, landscape to landscape. My reading walk leads nowhere, but it maps what writers have woven between us. A book is a road.

The first time I attempted graduate school, I posted a large, white, empty cardboard on my living room wall. My intention was to trace the genealogy of Quebec women writers. I had been taught that many of them had a writing practice in the spheres (and genres) reserved to women: the intimate, the domestic. Many never published, but they kept journals, corresponded with one another, mentored younger authors. They read one another, encouraged each other; they took their literary work seriously. Thus, all the women published in the nineteenth and twentieth centuries in Quebec—as exceptional as they seemed, as if they'd sprung out of nowhere—benefited from an intellectual network. To reveal this network, I began searching the family archives of the era's thinkers, following the tracks of each correspondent.

I was obsessed by this hidden network. I saw it as the groundwork, as the foundation that allowed these pioneers to speak out, as a safeguard for those already publishing, as the condition required to create literature, history. Was this how writing was done? Not only by addressing God or posterity but in response to peers and friends? This web of correspondence allowed me to perceive literary negatives: the hidden participation of muses, secretaries, and mothers. So many missing women! I absolutely had to show this map to the rest of the world! But every time I approached the board to scrawl a name, my hand hovered indefinitely. Each name seemed linked to all the others—at once inheritor, companion, and ancestor of so many other texts. Where to begin? My web of those who had disappeared extended so far (into the entire history of thought) that I wasn't able to reveal any part of it, to the great amusement of my roommates at the time, who tolerated this enormous, invisible cartography in the midst of our apartment. "What's that big, white thing on your wall?" "Oh, that's Val's 'project.'"

One day, having never written a single name on the board, I took it down. But I didn't stop searching. As a feminist editor, I kept following in the footsteps of these hidden correspondents. I spent sleepless nights each time I stumbled across another woman journalist who'd debated with anarchists and heads of state, another brilliant lover to whom male poets and philosophers had dedicated antagonistic works, or a concert organizer who got revolutionary songstresses to share now-forgotten stages, singers who were never anthologized. I've often seen other feminists attempt this cartography of the invisible. It's what Louky Bersianik* did.

It's what I witnessed when I went to the Brooklyn Museum with a few friends and we were all overcome with emotion upon seeing Judy Chicago's *Dinner Party*.[1] There are treasures on this walk. I'm always surprised when I meet people who only stroll along the main boulevards, who only read the pretentious and serious works of "history." Everyone knows that to really experience a city, you've got to roam its alleys.

I'm never alone on this walk. The first iteration of this essay was published in the online journal *Raisons sociales*,† which is now defunct, but where you can still find traces of the conversations we had among "comrades." The journal, which published fiction and essays alike, attempted to cross disciplines and voices, to leverage our friendships so that we might together think outside our own furrows. I contributed a few literary and feminist pieces, but I was always hoping my friends, who were better trained in the social sciences than me, might provide answers to some of my questions. But while my ideas were generously and enthusiastically welcomed, we

* Louky Bersianik (1930–2011): Lucile Durand, known as Louky Bersianik, was a Quebec activist, novelist, poet, and essayist. She was the author of the celebrated novel *L'Euguélionne*, the first major feminist Quebec novel. A nonprofit feminist cooperative bookstore in Montreal was named L'Euguélionne in the author's honour.

† *Raisons sociales*: A Quebec online literary, history, and criticism journal (raisons-sociales.com) that ran from 2013–2019. The publication was archived in 2021.

shared little vocabulary. As with any mixed editorial collective, the project required a lot of humour and a high tolerance for the ineffable. I had hoped that our desire to work together would enable us to, despite ourselves, broaden our perspectives. I didn't publish much there, but I often said it was where I could be read; it was as if I had a home.

I name many women on this walk, beginning with those who made me look at my own power within the literary institution. But we can imagine the footprints left by all kinds of different conversations. A longtime friend who's constantly challenging me when she shares poems by Louise Michel* or translations of women writers from Rojava. Others who have agreed to read and help me, those whose work feeds on political science and literature. The friend who finally stopped being her professor's secretary; the one who overcame the most violent prohibitions on free speech; the one who got angry for me; the one I still hope will write. Everyone who's taught me something—sometimes by instructing me but more often by welcoming me and treating me as an interlocutor, an equal. The friend who convinced me I should still believe in debating ideas; the one who, in Budapest, showed me Soviet vestiges before their demolition; the involuntary devil's advocate who tossed my nonconformism back in my face every time I let my guard down; the philosophy

* Louise Michel (1830–1905): Dubbed the "French grande dame of anarchy" by journalist Brian Doherty, Louise Michel was a teacher and public figure who spoke on anarchism across Europe and was the first, in 1883, to wave a black flag at a demonstration. The flag would later be known as the anarchist black flag.

prof who never responded to my criticism publicly but who assigned my essays to his students, and who, even today, tries to find the common ground between us.

Friendship is revolutionary. It cultivates curiosity over differences, fosters solidarity in discord. The friendship between men and women ends the classic division between the speaker and their muse. It's one way women may accompany someone without themselves disappearing. Friendship doesn't wither with distance; it's there when it's called on. It's generative, a performative utterance. I say, "my comrades," and I'm no longer perceived as a solitary walker. Suddenly, you're here, walking beside me on this overgrown path, where a few statue heads are scattered. I add my map to yours.

You might find, in this text, traces of my own revolt against my erasure. Reactions to all those who've asked me what man I was there with; to those who've refused to shake my hand or look me in the eye; to those who've explained how feminism is just a side project or that my literary approach is counterrevolutionary; and to those who didn't recognize my name even if I'd rewritten their books. While writing feeds on adversity, it can also bypass adversity to seek friendships further afield. Writing can overcome our first interlocuters' rejections. This text is my response to a British biographer, to anonymous Communards. I want to say that the answer won't be where you think it'll be. Some young women recently wrote to me from across the sea. They were trying to make their literary magazine a more egalitarian space. They'd read one of my essays, "*Faire parler les muses*," ("Giving the Muses the Floor") in the 2014 anthology *Sexe, amour et pouvoir à l'université* (*Sex, Love and Power in the University*)[2] and they wanted to express their discouragement to me. What they didn't know was how timely their writing to me was; that they were *my* answer. They were weaving a web that won't let itself be erased. This is what books do: they forge their own friendships. A text might not show up where you've called it, but it will travel without you, and it calls to people who will carry you even further.

The way my friends at Les Éditions du remue-ménage* do.

The one who walks is a caravan.

* Les Éditions du remue-ménage: A Quebec publisher founded in 1976 by a woman's collective specialized in publishing feminist works. "*Remue-ménage*" means "commotion" in French.

# Jenny, Eleanor, and Laura, et al.

## This Is Not a Book About Marx

I'm angry at myself (and at certain literary institutions) for the same reason at regular intervals. The summer before this walk began, for example, Marie-Eveline Belinga* got me to read Suzanne Césaire.† I didn't know who she was. As a literature student, I'd loved Césaire—*Aimé* Césaire.‡ I mean, I learned the beginning of *Cahier d'un retour au pays natal* (*Journal of a Homecoming*)[3] by heart because it felt so good to shout it out loud. I return to him often to reflect on the different contexts of decolonialization, such as how it impacts Québécois literature or feminism. But I never knew that his wife wrote. No one teaches us

* Marie-Eveline Belinga: Of Cameroonian and Quebec origin, Marie-Eveline Belinga grew up in Senegal. Belinga's work focuses on practices of oral transmission and African philosophical heritage.

† Suzanne Césaire (1915–1966): A writer and intellectual from Martinique, Suzanne Césaire's writing focused on feminism, surrealism, and anti-imperialism. She and her spouse, Aimé Césaire, founded the magazine *Tropiques*.

‡ Aimé Césaire (1913–2008): An author, poet, and politician from Martinique, Aimé Césaire was one of the founders of the Négritude movement in Francophone literature. In 1958, he founded the Parti progressiste Martiniquais and served in the French National Assembly from 1945–1993. He was the president of Martinique's Regional Council from 1983–1988 and was the mayor of Fort-de-France from 1945–2001. He was married to Suzanne Césaire.

that—that women write. No one ever says, Oh, by the way, did you know that Suzanne Césaire wasn't content to just hold literary salons? She was a committed editor, a perceptive and courageous author (as revealed by the select texts that have trickled our way despite the colonialist obstacles to the dissemination of French-language literature). A couple of days later, Stéphane Martelly* was telling me about the critical importance of Mireille Neptune Anglade's† writing. I—who had worked with her spectacular husband, Georges Anglade‡—had no idea. But I know how it goes. As an editor, I'm trained to look for the forgotten women writers (who can be found in droves among the mistresses of those writers we have not at all forgotten). I should I have known. I should have been curious. I should have read Mireille Neptune Anglade and Suzanne Césaire. You could ask me at any moment what I'm currently angry about and I'd tell you about some other writer who's never been

* Stéphane Martelly: Born in Haiti, the writer, painter, translator, and scholar now lives in Montréal where she is an affiliate professor in the Theatre Department and Main Coordinator for the Centre of Oral History and Digital Storytelling at Concordia University.

† Mireille Neptune Anglade (1944–2010): Born in Haiti and educated at the Sorbonne, Mireille Neptune Anglade was a militant feminist, writer, and intellectual who spent much of her life in Quebec. Much of her research, writing, and work with the United Nations focused on the working conditions and status of women in Haiti. She was married to Georges Anglade.

‡ Georges Anglade (1944–2010): Born in Haiti and educated at Strasbourg, Georges Anglade was a geographer, politician, writer, and one of the founders of UQAM—the Université du Québec à Montréal. He was an activist for Haitian democracy from his residences both in Quebec and Haiti. He was married to Mireille Neptune Anglade.

on my radar—I bet you'd learn something, too. And yet, contaminated as we are by centuries of theoretical misogynist jokes, don't think for a second I'm insinuating that genius is transferred by osmosis to women by the touch (by the seed) of these great men. It's much simpler than that. I find women writers among the male writers' mistresses because writing is done communally. There are, of course, some truly solitary author figures, but in the vast majority of cases, contrary to common tropes, writing is done by corresponding with, talking to, and reading one another. Since women have been historically deprived of intellectual networks, they have written within their family contexts, and this in addition to having often served as secretaries, muses, and editors, labouring in the shadows. These muses, who didn't benefit from reciprocal editorial support, leave us fragmented works, often too thin for ordinary publishers to consider. But to me, these fragments are essential to the history of ideas and criticism. They are an extension of every literary school of thought. Decolonialization was also, and remains, a feminist principle (Quebec's feminist activists spoke compellingly of this once upon a time, ecofeminists still do today). I don't know how women intellectuals in Martinique have wrestled with the question. I need to read Marie-Eveline's thoughts on Suzanne Césaire, as well as other authors who have been forgotten, or silenced. A few weeks after these discussions, while watching the trailer for the 2017 film *Le Jeune Karl Marx* (*The Young Karl Marx*),[4] I was shaken by the representation of Karl's wife, Jenny Marx. Jenny participating in debates, Jenny in the press, Jenny the editor. I was in shock. Had I neglected yet another muse? Many people in my social circle studied political or social sciences—they can teach classes on the works of Karl Marx. But no one had ever bothered to mention the intellectual oeuvre of the woman who'd accompanied him his entire life. And yet it's not surprising. Clearly a concept of the magnitude of Marxism must have relied upon—and been deeply rooted in—a powerful network. And this group, which transformed the world, notably for its feminist ideas, included women.

Obviously.

"Come on, the real poetry is elsewhere. Far from rhymes, complaints, trade winds, parrots. Bamboos, we decree the death of cuddly literature. And damn hibiscus, frangipane, bougainvillea. Martinican poetry will be cannibalistic, or it will not be."

—Suzanne Césaire[5]

"The strictly Marxist approach to the question refers this concern to one of many secondary contradictions (such as the national question, the colour question, the religion question, etc.) that the advent of communism would dissolve, since, as Engels supports, it is capitalism that created them in their systems of contemporary contradiction. But 'domestic slavery' has resisted this proclaimed end, like the question of colour, like the national question, like the religion question."

—Mireille Neptune Anglade[6]

So I went looking for them. Stage one of my investigation: consulting with Marxist friends. The friends who hung sepia portraits (which occasionally served as mirrors), dolls, or dartboards with an effigy of Karl in their living rooms. Or those decked out in heavy metal or retro Christmas T-shirt likenesses of the man. And the friends who lectured sagely on Marxism. At great lengths. Passionately. The folks who owned, among their arsenal of such tools, *The Young Karl Marx*,[7] and whipped it out at the least occasion. I asked them: What do you know of the work of Eleanor Marx? Of the impact of Jenny Marx's or Laura Marx's influence on Karl Marx? I asked my comrades at *Raisons sociales* if anyone, over their copious years of education, had even uttered their names?

Their answers were even more evasive than I'd have imagined. Maybe it was bad timing. When this essay first circulated online, I told my friends: Throw everything you've got at me. But that's not what happened. Several political science professors wrote to me to congratulate me and to request more information on Eleanor. At least I could laugh when I answered them, "But *you're* the specialist!"

What I mostly heard was that these women led "quite sad lives." Dead children, poverty, illness, abandonment, self-centred or violent spouses, exile, suicide . . . Welcome to the Marxes. And yet, my understanding is that the lives of the Marx women were not so wretched.

In stage two of my investigation, I wandered the internet ad hoc, and I found some signs of life. In a famous photo of the Marx couple, Jenny stares, with conviction, beyond the frame. She looks as stern as her husband, which is saying a lot. She was, they say, the only person who could stand up to him, but that's typical lore when it comes to the legitimate wife archetype. The same was said of Helene Demuth, also known as "Lenchen," who worked as the Marxes' governess—a fact that should probably be revisited. I think of Xanthippe.* It's striking that the Marx women, while they have not been granted respect or recognition for their intellectual work, have not been ridiculed by Marxist historians. I'm not going so far as to say that the history of intellectual thought admits it owes anything to the Marx women. But the fact that they're not described as annoyances—in accordance with a certain literary tradition—seems worthy of mention. No complete works translated into twenty languages exist for these women intellectuals. I was happy to stumble across *Lettres d'amour et de combat* (*Letters of Love and Struggle*)[8] by Karl and Jenny Marx (with an introduction by Jacques-Olivier Bégot†). What first struck me about this slim book was the lightness with which the publishers treated Jenny's contribution to these correspondences. The publishers neglected to mention (on the cover or on the title page) that the book reveals a substantial chunk

* Xanthippe (fifth–fourth century BCE): An Ancient Athenian, Socrates' wife, and mother to their three sons, Xanthippe was described in Xenophon's *Symposium* as "the most difficult, harshest, painful, ill-tempered wife." This characterization of her temperament has endured in portrayals of her in the arts and literature since.

† Jacques-Olivier Bégot: A writer and lecturer at the Université Paris-Diderot–Paris VII, Jacques-OlivierBégot teaches philosophy and aesthetics.

Xanthippe, Socrates' wife, has become the archetype of the shrew who prevents Socrates from philosophizing with her salutary chamber pot. The Greek philosopher and historian Xenophon has Socrates say: "What matters most to me is the art of living with men: it is this woman that I have taken, certain that, if I could bear her, I should get along easily with everyone." I always keep a mental chamber pot in reserve for those who think that philosophizing requires cutting oneself off from the world and young children, for those who think that making fun of wives' worries makes them seem greater. Source: Emblemata d'Otto van Veen, 1607 – *Wikimedia Commons*

of Jenny's autobiography. Bégot, although a Marxist specialist, doesn't seem to be aware of the existence of certain classically sexist biases. Of these letters, Bégot writes that they are "certainly less demanding" than Marx's other correspondents. He doesn't bother to translate Jenny's Latin quotes (content to consider them incomprehensible), and yet she was a funny polyglot, prone to puns and inventive translations. Bégot was, of course, first and foremost addressing Marxist specialists, and I must at least be grateful that he proffered the following scandalous hypothesis: Jenny may have been much more than just a secretary(!).

What's left a lasting impression on me, throughout my research, is Jenny's personality. Her anger, her love, her vivacity, her recognizably acid humour, which she liberally lavished on her semi-allies and timid, right-thinking sheep alike. Jenny poked fun at everyone, including herself. When she complained about her condition as a woman, therefore, it was with neither pretention nor hope. She admitted to being torn between her ideals and the constraints of her everyday life. She judged herself with a certain dash of cynicism; a derision that could be cruel when reflected inward but turned to revolt when it came to her daughters.

Jenny teased her husband as she did everyone else, but this teasing is not itself quite criticism. Her laughter was the chortle of a strong personality defying the storm—a matter of survival. She willingly devoted herself to Karl's work. She supported him in every aspect of his life. As his editor, translator, lover, caregiver, negotiator, watchdog . . . What has come down to us from her are these letters addressed to Karl and to their children. While her

Portrait of Jenny von Westphalen. Source: Date and artist unknown – *Wikipedia Commons*

Source: Date and photographer unknown – *Wikipedia Commons*

Of these photos, which have gone down in history as representing a great man pleasantly accompanied by a woman, we only know that the woman pictured is *a* Jenny. But which Jenny? Daughter? Mother? Jenny Marx Longuet or Jenny von Westphalen Marx? Publications affirm both, both online and in print alike.

Source: Date and photographer unknown – *Wikipedia Commons*

Because of my research, I feel that I can say, at the time of publication, that Jenny the daughter is pictured in the photo with the pale dress, and Jenny the mother is in the photo with the black dress. My editor at Remue-ménage, however, believes the opposite is true.

revolutionary impulse is beyond doubt, her particularly feminist revolt remains somewhat shadowed. I am nonetheless struck by her lucidity regarding domestic work and the humility imposed upon women, which leads only to a form of resignation. I don't know what to think, for example, of this passage from a letter she wrote in her youth, in which Jenny hinted at her frustration at not being able to write:

> If only I could level and smooth all these paths for you, make room for everything that might stand in your way. But that is not our lot, we must not energetically meddle with the wheels of fate. We are condemned to passivity by original sin, by the fault of Mrs. Eve, and our lot is to wait, to hope, to endure, and to suffer. At most, we have been entrusted with the task of knitting stockings—needles and keys—and anything beyond that is evil; it is only when it is a question of determining where to print the *Deutsche Jahrbrücher** that a female veto can be invoked, and that it plays, without being seen, a small yet important part.[9]

If Jenny participated in feminist reflection within the Marx coterie, her writing suggests that it was laced with bitterness. Her writing reveals a woman broken by tragedies—including the deaths of three children—who sometimes hoped her surviving daughters might find an alternative to marriage. She also divulges a remarkable

* *Deutsch–Französische Jahrbücher* (German: *German French Annals*): A single volume of this publication, a double-issue, came out in 1844. It included Karl Marx's essay "On the Jewish Question" and Friedrich Engels' "Outline of a Critique of Political Economy."

sense of clannishness. Faithful and generous in her friendships, despite the hardships of her era, it is she who shows the Marxes to be a family of thinkers.

Freedom in love has often been central to revolutionary debates, and Jenny had inevitably seen and heard it all in this raucous house where she crossed paths with writers, politicians, and activists from all walks of life. The fragments of her memoir, published in *Letters of Love and Struggle*,[10] mentioned that August Willich,* who had moved in with the Marxes, had a theory of "natural" communism, which, apparently, would "draw out the worm that lurks in every marriage." A year later, August challenged Karl to a duel on the grounds of the latter not being radical enough. Jenny didn't say more on the subject, but I found myself hoping she'd had a few caring lovers throughout her festive, well-travelled life. An undoubtedly anachronistic thought, since sexual freedom for Jenny would have entailed more indescribably severe consequences for her than for him. We do know that she wanted this freedom for her daughters, and that she tolerated it in her home—but in a way the taboos of the time didn't let her address directly.

Jenny was an avid reader—as passionate about political debates as she was about literature. She led an independent career as an intellectual. We know that she taught at the university, and that she wrote

* August Willich (1810–1878): Johann August Ernst von Willich was born into Prussian nobility. He gave up his title in 1847 and participated in 1848 European revolutions, also known as the "springtime of the peoples." An early proponent of communism, he disagreed with Karl Marx, whom he found too conservative. Willich emigrated to the United States and served in the Union Army during the American Civil War (1861–1865).

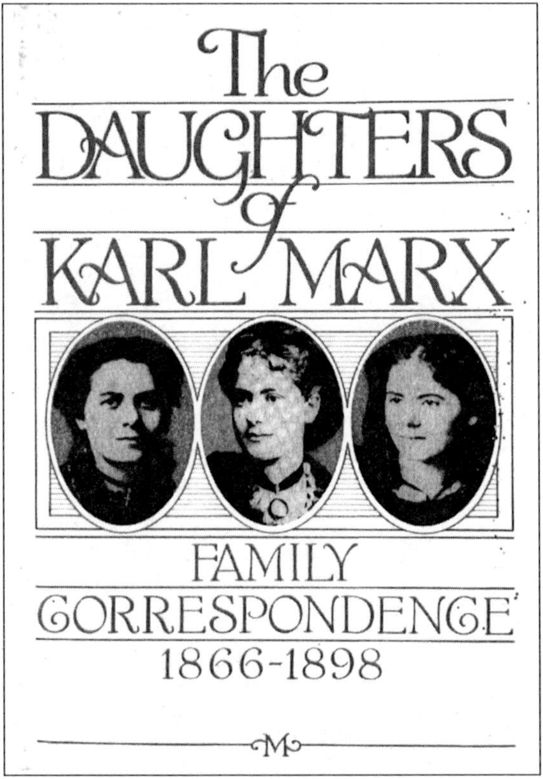


The cover of Jenny Marx Longuet, Laura Marx Lafargue, and Eleanor Marx Aveling's *The Daughters of Karl Marx: Family Correspondence, 1866–1898*, which was published in 1982 by Harcourt Brace Jovanovich.

theatre reviews. But she spent most of her life working as a researcher, transcriber, editor, and proofreader for her husband and his friends. Often to the detriment of her family's convenience and comfort. When an envoy of the Prussian government arrived to investigate the home of this notoriously dangerous family, what seems to have most scandalized him was not what the revolutionaries said but rather Jenny and Helene's lamentable housekeeping skills, as well as the presence of the Marx children during the most passionate and debaucherous discussions, which he would have preferred were conducted only among men.

I found an amusing anecdote among some correspondences. A letter from Jenny was edited and published by Karl Marx and his friends in *Vorwärts*.* Without her approval. It's an excellent letter, very much in Jenny's biting style, but better, constructed as a manifesto. It was, I thought, a perfect letter. Then I understood what had been edited. They had removed any of her inevitable passages about family, or quotidian hardships. Jenny always shared news of her children, of Karl's mother, of friends. She constantly alternated between the harsh realities of her everyday life and the demanding philosophical and political considerations (with apologies to the publisher). There was always a critical richness to what these appositions implied, a sometimes-brutal collage of political ideals and disappointing compromises. In short, to publish her letter, the editors had purged it of its multidimensionality,

* *Vorwärts* (German: *Forward*): A newspaper founded in 1876 and published by the Social Democratic Party of Germany (SPD).

rendering it more readable for the review's audience but at the same time amputating half of its political relevance.

This letter is a metaphor for our truncated reading of the world and the erasure it demands.

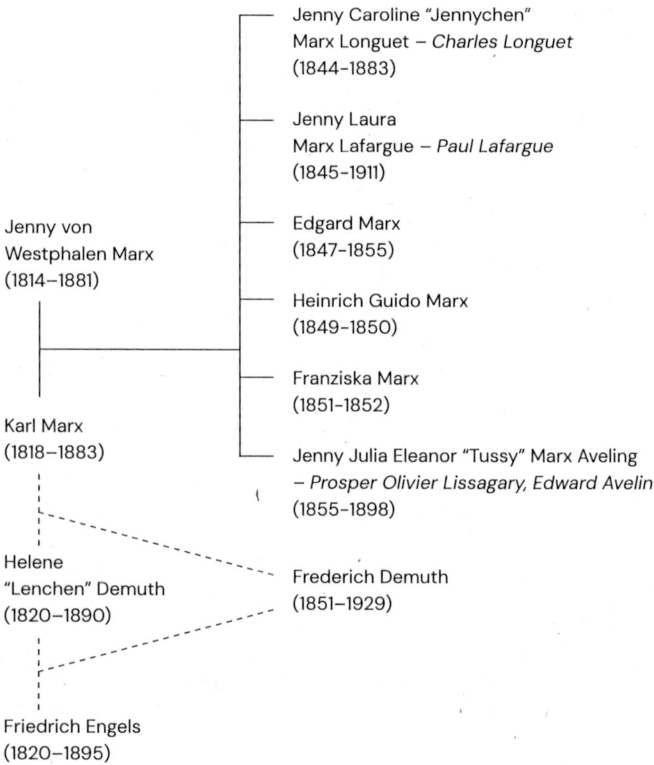

## Laura, Jennychen, Lenchen, and the Others

My research was intuitive; it followed winding paths. There's nothing straightforward about looking for the women of history—promising roads often lead to dead ends. Laura Marx Lafargue's almost empty Wikipedia page tells us that she translated *The Communist Manifesto*[11] into French, which even today remains a significant contribution. (I note that in the Aden edition, which was based on Laura's original translation, the text was initially unsigned. How interesting, it was presented as a collective work, based on the Communist League's* ideas. I'm not the only one seeing more than three people around the table at the time of writing.) The Marx daughters spoke perfect French—especially the two eldest, Jenny and Laura, who had spent a good part of their childhoods in France and Belgium. The youngest, Eleanor, was more of a Londoner (and Irish at heart). Jennychen is also the forbearer of some famous personalities of French artistic and political life at the time. Early on in my research, I told myself quite naively that I could find traces of them throughout the French edition of the book (but at this stage there was much I didn't yet understand about Marxist publishers).

Erudite, polyglot, and steadfast activists, the three Marx sisters were shaped by a prodigious parade of original personalities and brilliant minds. The most present in the Marx household was undoubtedly their

* The Communist League (German: *Bund der Kommunisten)*: Established in 1847 in London, the international political party was formed by merging the League of the Just and the Communist Correspondence Committee. Karl Marx and Friedrich Engels wrote the *Communist Manifesto* in 1847 on behalf of the group, considered the first Marxist political party.

"godfather" Friedrich Engels and sisters Mary and Lizzie Burns.* (As I mention the Burns women, I realize this parenthesis cannot end here. Mary steals the show in Peck's film, *The Young Karl Marx*.[12] It was said, of Friedrich's great love, that she introduced him to the reality of the working class, and it was said of Lizzie, her younger sister, that she introduced him to feminism.) The Marx daughters also took turns working as their father's secretaries. Their specialized and free labour apparently allowed Karl Marx to see to their education, thereby circumventing the dumbing down of girls in the regular school system.

Only the youngest of the three daughters could occasionally shrug off the burden of caring for children, the sick, husbands, and the dead and thus lead an independent intellectual and political career. Laura Marx Lafargue and Jenny Marx Longuet, like their mother, shouldered a significant domestic load that inevitably checked their voices. They both married, despite their father's grumblings, French writers and activists (the love for Communards didn't spare the youngest daughter, but she still ducked marriage) and the more I find traces of them in historical texts, the more they seem to me to be at the heart of the dissemination of their father's ideas in France. You can imagine the Marx daughters, still incredibly young,

* Mary Burns (1821–1863) and Lydia "Lizzie" Burns (1827–1878): The two Manchester Irish sisters were intelligent though illiterate working-class women. Both were romantically involved with Friedrich Engels and are credited for showing him the actual conditions of British factory employees.

The Marx family's two eldest daughters, Jenny and Laura Marx, about 1865. Source: Photographer unknown – *Wikimedia Commons*

invited by Elisabeth Dmitrieff* to *l'Union des femmes pour la défense de Paris et les soins aux blessés* (*The women's union for the defense of Paris and care for the wounded*), meeting Nathalie Lemel,† Louise Michel, in love with men and the revolution alike, deciding to stay in France, to translate the Communards writings, to try to find shelter for the exiled.

Jennychen died tragically when she was only thirty-eight years old, exhausted by successive pregnancies and illnesses, following a catastrophic sixth delivery. Laura is still shadowed by her husband in French memory. And yet her life wasn't without its twists and turns. Laura played a significant role in the famous family's courage. She famously searched for her husband while fleeing the police through the Pyrenees, a dying baby at her breast—this is a story Jennychen told in a letter published in 1871. She and Eleanor, who was only sixteen at the time, were detained and interrogated by the police (who were unable to gain any information), while peasants from the Pyrenees helped the Lafargues escape. She writes:

In other parts of France, I have since heard that the

* Elisabeth Dmitrieff (1850–unknown, estimated to be from 1916 to 1918): A Russian revolutionary and feminist activist, Elisabeth Dmitrieff, born Elizaveta Lukinichna Kusheleva, was the illegitimate daughter of a German nurse and a Russian aristocrat. She studied in Geneva, where she helped found the Swiss chapter of the International Workingmen's Association. Dispatched to London for the organization, she became close to the Marx family, particularly with Karl Marx's daughter, Jenny.

† Nathalie Lemel (1827–1921): Formally trained as a bookbinder, Nathalie Lemel was known for her militant anarchist feminism. A participant at the barricades at the Commune de Paris in 1871, she was deported, alongside Louise Michel, to Nouvelle Calédonie.

> peasants are quite as much opposed to their *so-called* representatives, the governing Rurals. M. Thiers fulfills a great revolutionary mission! By means of his prefects, priests, *garde champêtres*, and gendarmes he will before long provoke a general rising of the peasantry![13]

Laura lived a long time after the rest of her family had died and therefore had more time to write, translate, and edit the family works. We owe a lot to her. But, like her mother, she devoted herself to the writing of others. Curiously, French publishing history seems to have erased her contribution, despite the fact that correspondences prove she actively participated in the writing, translation, and publication of several major works in French.

The Lafargues gathered at their table, like the Marx parents, an eclectic mix of political figures and writers. If we're not sticklers for staying in our respective activist lanes, it would be worthwhile to research these friendships, particularly the presence of several French anarchists, British feminists, Russian socialists . . . I read everywhere that their friend, Alexandra Kollontai*—a sometimes erased link between anarcha-feminism and Marxism (and champion for the cause of free love for

* Alexandra Kollontai (1872–1952): A Russian revolutionary, politician, and diplomat. Alexandra Kollontai, a Marxist theoretician, served as the People's Commissar for Welfare in Lenin's government from 1917–1918. A prominent figure in the Bolshevik party, she was the first woman to be a cabinet minister and the first woman ambassador.

women!)—delivered a eulogy for Paul Lafargue at the Père-Lachaise cemetery* before thousands of mourners.

It is not often said that it was a double funeral. Laura committed suicide alongside Paul Lafargue, in accordance with his plan to die before he turned seventy, leaving historians with troubling suspicions about her own intentions.

A curious character in this family continues to attract attention, even without having left any written traces. Helene Demuth was born into a peasant family in 1820—the same year as Friedrich Engels—and went into domestic service at eight years old, an experience said to have been traumatic. As an adolescent, she was hired by the von Westphalen family to work as Jenny's governess. There, she was better treated, received an education, and was integrated into the family—becoming like a sister to Jenny Marx, whom she would follow all her life, even to the family grave. I read that in addition to keeping house, Helene assisted with the family editorial labour and continued to aid Friedrich Engels in his work after Karl Marx's death.

Nothing is known of Helene Demuth's own thoughts or voice, but we are aware of the love the Marx children bore for her, as well as the fact that she triggered, particularly in Eleanor's work, reflections and criticism on the subject of domestic work and the status of women. How can socialists campaign for the emancipation of all

* Père-Lachaise Cemetery: The largest cemetery in Paris, Père-Lachaise Cemetery is the most visited cemetery in the world. Notable figures buried there include Colette, Frédéric Chopin, Édith Piaf, Marcel Proust, Georges Méliès, Sarah Bernhardt, Oscar Wilde, and Jim Morrison.

This photo was circulated to depict Helene Demuth, probably around 1850, before Frederick was born. Some sources date this photo to 1876 and hypothesize that it is a photograph of Mary Ellen Georgina Burns (known as "Pumps"), a notable niece of Lizzie and Mary Burns and an important figure in this extended family. You might consider the potential resemblances between the two women. Source: Photograph by Eduard Schultze – *Wikimedia Commons*

women if they need a domestic worker to do so? Today's feminists are far from having solved this unwieldy issue, which still preoccupies us with good reason. And how should the reproductive burden and care for humans be distributed in an egalitarian system? Another issue Helene "Lenchen" raised for Eleanor Marx was that of unequal sexual freedom between the sexes—and between women—and the effect these inequalities have upon children.

Historians have debated whether Helene's son Frederick was or wasn't Karl Marx's, a comical quarrel that reminds us of those areas where mothers are more competent than experts. Everyone seems to find it *plausible* that Karl was Frederick's father; that they looked very convincingly alike. Legend has it that Friedrich Engels confirmed the fact to Eleanor on his deathbed. But the child still bore the name Engels and grew up believing that Friedrich Engels was his father. I can draw a few hypotheses. Either sleeping with the boss and his cronies was part of a housekeeper's duties in the Marx household, which, while it wouldn't have been so out of the ordinary, nonetheless casts an unsightly shadow on some rather lovely theories (all the more challenging as Frederick's birth came at a time of great poverty and distress in the Marx family, which witnessed the death of two infants in 1850 and again in 1852). Or else Lenchen was simply a female participant in the group—a collaborator, a mistress, and a friend. And when you read Rachel Holmes's[14] biography of Eleanor, it's certainly a seductive hypothesis.

But some uncertainty remains, especially given Jenny's (Jenny the mother) anger at the child's birth, Eleanor's revolt when she learned the "truth," and the poor boy's general exclusion from the family. Eleanor was outraged by the injustice done to this half-brother, who had been hidden from her. Frederick, in fact, as the maid's natural son, was never able to benefit from the incredible education lavished upon the other Marx children and neither could he count on Engels's financial support—though Engels so often supported the Marxes, the Lafargues, and the Longuets. (Engels, a great feminist, said, at some point, of his wife, "My wife was a true daughter of the Irish proletariat, and her fierce loyalty to her class of origin meant far more to me—and helped me more in difficult times—than all the elegance of an educated middle-class bluestocking artist."[15] After all, didn't he himself theorize that in marriage, men are the bourgeois?) If Lenchen did not leave behind any work, her story is still engraved in my memory. Someplace that sticks.

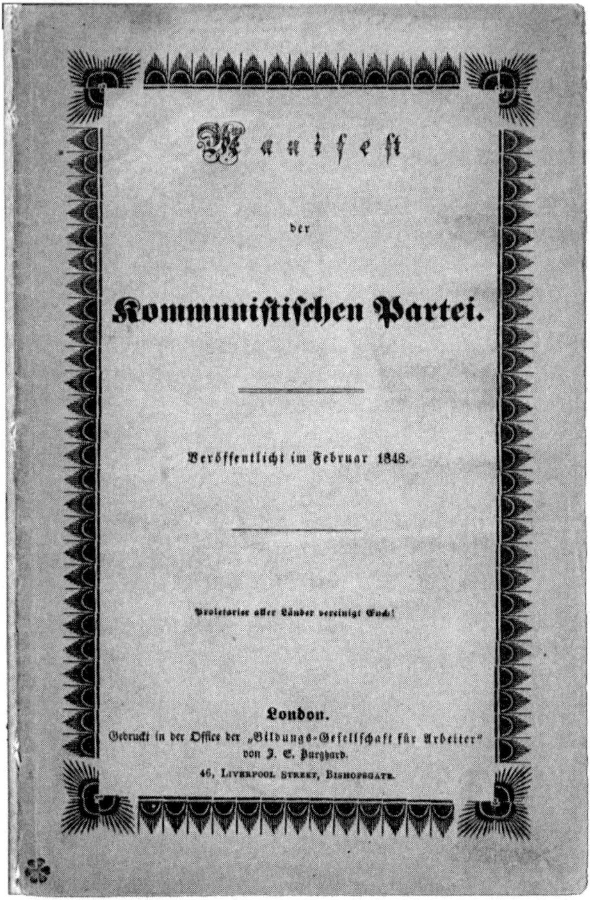


The cover of the first edition of Marx and Engels' 1848 *Manifest der Kommunistischen Partei*, published originally by the Workers Educational Association.

## Eleanor ("Tussy")

All the women in this story have left lasting impressions, like mythological heroines. But ever since I encountered Eleanor, the youngest of the Marx daughters, she's possessed me like a spectre; she follows me in my daily activities. She materializes in the hallway, decked in her dirty, uncorsetted old dresses, her hair a mess, with her pince-nez glasses and her actress' voice, to distract me from conversations and chores, to bellow at me to get my ass in gear—a veritable romantic author's inspiration. Just writing a couple of sentences about her, I can already see myself reflected in her oval portrait, proclaiming myself a Marxist "with Tussist leanings." A myth without a statue, substantive as Woolf or Bersianik, Eleanor dwells in me like some long-gone, irreplaceable grandmother. She also struck the imagination of her British contemporaries, including many writers, which seems to give the Marx daughters a little more resonance in the English-speaking world. What can be said about Eleanor in a few lines? That certain history books must be rewritten? Her biography, by Rachel Holmes,[16] reads like an adventure novel (for geeks). Not only was she involved in all the major political battles of her time, but she also expressed sound literary judgment, winsome charm, an extraordinary erudition, and an almost innate understanding of the works of Karl Marx and his colleagues. Her courage, generosity, and willpower seemed limitless, except where they concerned one person—herself. She had, in fact, a proven tendency towards self-destruction and all the symptoms of "hysteria," which was most often diagnosed in ambitious young women of the time.

This romantic-looking child is sometimes identified as Laura Marx at fifteen and sometimes as Eleanor Marx at eighteen. Source: About 1860 – *Wikimedia Commons*

She had an absolutely incredible education—Karl Marx even seems to have written a large part of *Kapital* (*Capital*)[17] with his youngest child first at his knees, then at his side doing research—and nothing to predispose her to the temperament of a good and respectable housewife. She inherited her mother's gift of gab and her sense of clannishness. Holmes describes Eleanor as a tireless intellectual and a very influential politician who brought socialism into existence in England—alongside modern feminism.[18] Tussy would say that socialism was "little more than a literary movement." Writes Homes, "She took his movement from its visionary pages on to the streets and on to the political stage."[19] Nothing less.

What if Eleanor had been a man? The question very much interests the biographer. Holmes describes Marx the father as genuinely aware of gender inequalities, a feminist activist before his time. When Eleanor was born, he penned this cynical comment to Engels, "I could not of course write to the *Tribune* yesterday and could not either today or for some time in the future, for yesterday my wife has given birth to a bona fide traveller—unfortunately of the sex par excellence . . . Had it been a male the matter would have been more acceptable."[20] What Karl Marx could not have known on the day of his daughter's birth was that had she been born a boy, this child would have vied for his own mark in history so much that we would today be talking about the Marx*es*.

Eleanor might have gleaned the slightest legitimate historical recognition if she'd lived just a few more years. But she would have had to have broken up with Edward Aveling first, the miscreant who was her companion in

Eleanor Marx with Wilhelm Liebknecht and Edward Aveling in the United States in 1886. The daughter of the German delegate (was it Alice or Gertrud?) who accompanied Eleanor on this official tour does not appear in the photo. Source: Photographer unknown – *Wikimedia Commons*

battle, travel, and writing, as almost all historians would have liked her to. When we talk about Eleanor, it seems the appropriate stance is to be bewildered by her tragic love life, as if it was exceptional that a bold and creative woman, an activist for justice and freedom, would accept violence and humiliation in her intimate life. But it's the historians' astonishment that surprises me.

Sadly, Eleanor's life ended abruptly when she committed suicide at forty-three years old. Once again, it's hard to say if it was "out of love for" or "at the hands of" her abusive, con artist partner. She had spent an entire year lecturing tirelessly on socialism—a socialism that defended a clearly feminist vision. At a conference in Chicago in 1886, she declared:

> We are told that "the socialists want to have women in common." Such an idea is only possible in a society that considers women as a commodity. Today, alas, it is just that. Too often, she has to sell her femininity to feed herself. But for socialists, a woman is a human being, and therefore cannot be possessed in common, any more than a socialist society can accept slavery.[21]

Of the Marx clan, Eleanor was the most insistent feminist, making feminism a priority from her adolescence. She worked alongside international activists, as well as influencing her friends' and her parents' work. Her motto was: "work and independence." She was not much interested in the question of rights and suffrage; for Eleanor, the causes of the exploitation and domination of women were above all economic, and there were levers in socialism to improve the lot of *all* women. Thus, even if she could support and inspire middle-class women in their project of individual emancipation, Eleanor invited women to, above all, join unions and labour associations. She campaigned for girls' education (including sex education) and against child labour (see her and Aveling's damning opinion of child labour in their 1891 *Labour Movement in America*[22]). On her lecture tours, she reported not only on workers' struggles but also on their reality as mothers, on the terrible living conditions of families.

Eleanor discussed these ideas with those she was close with, and we know that she participated in the reflections that led to *The Origin of the Family, Private Property, and the State*,[23] a text that she then defended tooth and nail, seeking to have it recognized by both socialists and feminists alike. She continued the reflection in "The Woman Question,"[24] a text coauthored with her partner, Aveling, in which she considers marriage to be a financial transaction: "Marriages, as they are arranged and carried out, with all their attendant circumstances and consequences, seem to us, let us state frankly, worse than prostitution. To consider them sacred or moral is desecration." This rather short text should not be forgotten, especially as it advances very early on (1886) the grounds of women's desires and equality in sexuality. If this text did not change the appearance of classic Marxism, I do not for one second doubt that women thinkers like Kollontai were inspired by it, as they were inspired by Engels, to scandalize everyone (and Lenin) in turn by defending free love and contraception.

Eleanor was not only Marx's literary legatee, but also Engels's—the man she considered her second father—and it was Eleanor who was entrusted with the colossal task of treating, organizing, revising, and publishing their posthumous works, according to their wills. She participated in the collective translation of *Kapital* into English and was also her father's first biographer.[25] This, in addition to translating and commenting on works as varied as the story of the Communard Lissagaray,[*] *A Doll's House*,[26] and *Madame Bovary*.[27]

She dreamed of a career as an actress but instead devoted her life to the socialist struggle while earning a living as a teacher or a literary critic. (Like her mother, she left behind many theatre critics who blended political and aesthetic commentary.) When Eleanor was not teaching Shakespeare to working women or French to activists, she wrote to newspapers to defend Russian, German, and Irish—even occasionally anarchist—militants. She joined strike movements, participated in Workers' International and the Independent Labour Party, and helped found the Socialist League. She was at the heart of an international and interdisciplinary network that linked brilliant women with remarkable lives

* Hippolyte-Prosper-Olivier "Lissa" Lissagaray (1838–1901): A French journalist and speaker, Lissagaray was a Republican journalist and a revolutionary socialist who participated in the 1871 Paris Commune and is known for writing *History of the Paris Commune of 1871*. The book, published in 1876, is a definitive eyewitness account of the events and was translated by Eleanor Marx.

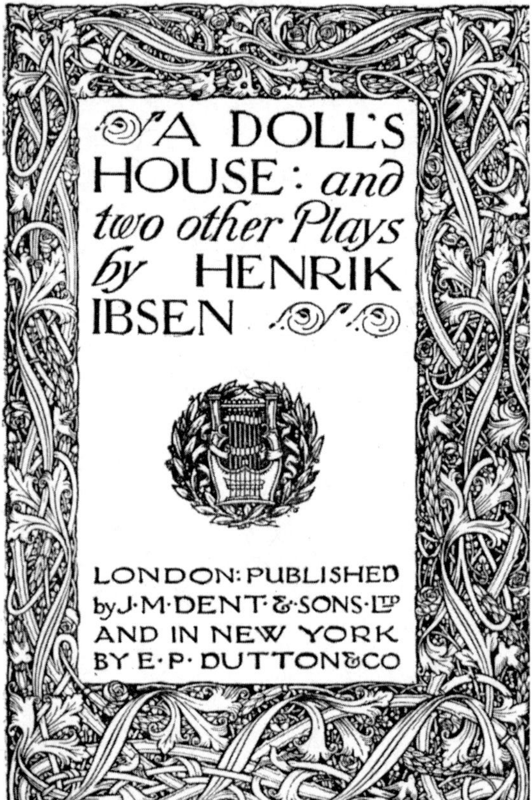


Eleanor Marx, who worked actively as a propagandist to unite men and women in the workers' struggle, did not stop at individual emancipation. Her choices as a translator prove that her feminism held more than an economic dimension. The cover of Henrik Ibsen's *A Doll's House and two other Plays*, translated by Eleanor Marx Aveling and R. Farquharson Sharp and published by Dent in 1910.

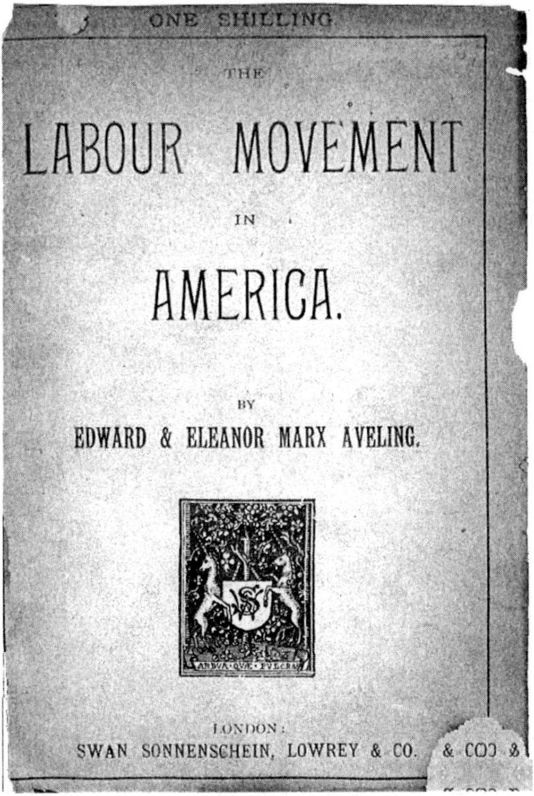


The cover of Edward Aveling and Eleanor Marx Aveling's 1888 book *The Labour Movement in America*, published by Swan Sonnenschein.

like Clara Zetkin,* Edith Lanchester,† Rosa Luxemburg,‡ and Olive Schreiner.§ As much as Eleanor resembled her father, she was the daughter of a company of women who contributed to her upbringing and strength—women like Jenny Marx, like Helene Demuth, and like Mary and Lizzie Burns. Eleanor, in turn, gave rise to women I will never again overlook. To follow her is to touch upon a vast fabric of women who speak out and change the world. Infinitely.

* Clara Zetkin (1857–1933): A German Marxist theorist and women's rights activist.

† Edith "Biddy" Lanchester (1871–1966): A British socialist and feminist, Biddy Lanchester rose to fame when, in 1895, her family had her institutionalized for planning to live with her Irish, working-class lover. Lanchester worked as Eleanor Marx's secretary.

‡ Rosa Luxemburg (1871–1919): A Polish and German revolutionary socialist, Rosa Luxemburg, born to a secular Jewish family, was also an orthodox Marxist and an antiwar activist during WWI. She was a member of the Proletariat party, the Social Democracy of the Kingdom of Poland and Lithuania, the Social Democratic Party of Germany, the Independent Social Democratic Party, the Partacus League, and the Communist Party of Germany.

§ Olive Schreiner (1855–1920): An author, antiwar activist, and intellectual from South Africa, Olive Schreiner is known for her novel *The Story of an African Farm* (1883) and for her later novel, published posthumously, *From Man To Man Or Perhaps Only* (1926).

This series of women also introduced me to Rachel Holmes.[28] As a feminist author and historian, she'd asked my questions before I had. She stopped for every female character of the revolution. She talks about men too, of course, but every woman who appears is, for her, someone to be celebrated. She's also written a book about Sylvia Pankhurst.* (Pankhurst's avant-garde feminism is notable for having argued, long before the 1970s, that the *private is political*. Holmes sparked this idea that the adolescent Sylvia and Tussy had met when the latter was already a famous political figure. In this scene, which Pankhurst never forgot, Aveling was rude to Eleanor in public, and she, the great feminist model, had responded with only a gentle gesture to protect Aveling. Pankhurst/Holmes makes this gesture the symbol of the impossible revolt, the capitulation of women on the second front.) Holmes has also written a biography of Saartjie Baartman,† the infamous woman who became a symbol of colonial violence (greed, stupidity, and misogyny) and researched

* Sylvia Pankhurst (1882–1960): The British feminist, socialist, and author was the daughter of Emmeline Pankhurst. Sylvia Pankhurst helped organize working-class women in London's East End. Supportive of Irish independence, she also an influential activist for anticolonialism throughout the British Empire. The book by Rachel Holmes is *Sylvia Pankhurst: Natural Born Rebel* (Bloomsbury Publishing, 2020).

† Sarah "Saartjie" Baartman (1789–1815): A Khoekhoe woman born in the Camdeboo Dutch Cape Colony, Saartjie Baartman was taken from her homeland and exhibited throughout Europe, where she was known as "Hottentot Venus." The extensive and invasive examination and fetishization of her body by scientists and the public—both when she was alive and after she died, at only twenty-six years old—speak to the brutal, dehumanizing, racist, and colonialist legacy of Europeans on the African continent.

Dr. James Barry,* a trans British woman considered to be the first woman doctor. (Dr. Barry was invited to Judy Chicago's table in the *Dinner Party*.[29])

This essay's crowding my table.

The walk has no end in sight. I could trace a path from Karl Marx to Emma Goldman on the Jewish question; from Eleanor Marx to the French Revolution by reading only women's poetry; I could delve into the Marx mother-daughter's thoughts on modern theatre; investigate their writer friends like Bernard Shaw† and Amy Levy‡ (I would like to read how Levy answered the first Marxist feminists on the subject of homosexuality). Each road branches off into another life, another work to discover. There isn't anything surprising about this; humans think and create together. Writing is a communal act. Philosophy is a forest.

But what's still surprising is the portrayal of Karl Marx alone in his frame. An entire family bore the name Marx. A joyful, supportive, funny, and idealistic clan of

* Dr. James Barry (1789–1865): A military surgeon in the British Army, James Barry, born in Cork, Ireland, graduated from the University of Edinburgh Medical School and worked as a doctor throughout the British Empire. Barry lived his entire adult life as a man, both publicly and privately, but was born Margaret Anne Bulkley.

† George Bernard Shaw (1856–1950): Born in Dublin, the Irish playwright, critic, and political activist moved to London in 1876. George Bernard Shaw is the author of over sixty plays, including *Pygmalion* (1913) and *Saint Joan* (1923). He was awarded the Nobel Prize in Literature in 1925.

‡ Amy Levy (1861–1889): A British essayist, poet, and novelist, Levy was the second Jewish woman to study at Cambridge University. Her writing, which included the novels *The Romance of a Shop* (1888) *and Reuben Sachs* (1888), touched on women's issues and Jewish culture. She died by suicide at twenty-seven years old. Oscar Wilde wrote a eulogy in *The Women's World* praising her literary gifts.

Eleanor Marx and Edward Aveling said of Clara Zetkin in Zürich at the 1893 International Workers' Congress: "Her position as a delegate is determined by the fact that whilst she was sent by the Social Democratic women of Mannheim, she was at the same time one of the great group of delegates sent by the whole party as a whole from Berlin. There is in that double delegation the whole question in a nutshell."[30] Source: Clara Zetkin and Rosa Luxemburg in Magdeburg in 1910 – Photographer unknown – *Wikimedia Commons*

"The indissoluble marriage based on the servitude of women is replaced by a free union of two equal members of the workers' state who are united by love and mutual respect. In place of the individual and egoistic family, a great universal family of workers will develop, in which all the workers, men and women, will above all be comrades. This is what relations between men and women, in the communist society will be like. These new relations will ensure for humanity all the joys of a love unknown in the commercial society of a love that is free and based on the true social equality of the partners."[31] Source: Alexandra Kollontai in 1900 – Photographer unknown – *Wikimedia Commons*

Marxes, who were passionate about literature and defying every authority. A gang of feminists. Why do we persist in upholding this image of the great man alone in his frame? I know everyone in this story admired Karl Marx. Engels tended to diminish the importance of their work in dialogue and put his brilliant friend before himself. But no one doubts the significance of this friendship and precisely how it created their work. Why don't we talk about the clan, about the collective action of thinking? Is it less serious because the whole family was involved? Influence flows both ways. The fact that Karl Marx and his posterity have benefited from so many brains does not take anything away from him; on the contrary—if the man was able to inspire and mobilize so many of his loved ones, it only makes him better to me.

A friend showed me pictures from her childhood, and they included this image of the statues, now in the Soviet Monument Cemetery in Budapest.* Karl Marx and Friedrich Engels stand square, dominant, stern. Emanating precisely what went off the rails in the communist adventure. Marx and Engels in granite, towering alone, undisturbed. But they were a family, a school, a hub, a popular revolution . . . What use is this isolation? Where does this need to extract men from living thought and turn them into immovable stars come from? Do we write to change the world? To touch other people? Or to worship statues? And what do we lose when we bet that an idea will go further if it is carried by a single man? What I like about Peck's film is the exercise of

* Soviet Monument Cemetery, Budapest: Since 1993, Memento Park has housed Hungary's fallen and toppled communist-era statues.

bringing thought back to life, into teeming discussions. When people talk to me about Marxism, I won't picture a stone bust. I will try to remember these images of Karl, Friedrich, Jenny, Mary, Jenny, Laura, and Eleanor, as well as a kind of dream, an alternative version, of being part of the gang.

And I would like other dimensions added to my creations, by reading Martelly (who has launched an imprint at Éditions du remue-ménage) and Belinga (whose works make me wonder now what the history of thought owes to the oral tradition); by thanking all of these people for their discoveries and their rage and for, like me, demanding a more accurate version of history by resisting the statue-fication of thought.

Karl Marx and Friedrich Engels at the entrance to Memento Park, in Budapest. Source: Photograph by Jorge Gobbi, 2012, *Flickr*.

# Notes

1. Judy Chicago, *The Dinner Party, 1974–79*. Ceramic, porcelain, textile, 576 × 576 in (1463 × 1463 cm). Brooklyn Museum; Gift of the Elizabeth A. Sackler Foundation, 2002.
2. Valérie Lefebvre-Faucher, *"Faire parler les muses,"* in *Sexe, amour et pouvoir: Il était une fois, à l'université*, ed. Martine Delvaux, Valérie Lebrun, and Laurence Pelletier (Les Éditions du remue-ménage, 2015), chapter 11.
3. Aimé Césaire, *Journal of a Homecoming*, trans. Irele Davis (Duke University Press, 2017).
4. Raoul Peck, dir., *Le Jeune Karl Marx*, France: Velvet Films, 2017, 118 min.
5. Suzanne Césaire, *The Great Camouflage: Writings of Dissent (1941–1945)*, ed. Daniel Maximin, trans. Keith L. Walker (Wesleyan University Press, 2012), 66.
6. Mireille Neptune Anglade, *L'autre moitié du développement: à propos du travail des femmes en Haïti* (Alizés/CIDIHCA, 1997), 36–37.
7. Peck, *Jeune Karl Marx*.
8. Karl Marx and Jenny Marx, *Lettres d'amour et de combat*, trans. Jacques-Olivier Bégot (Rivages poche, 2013).
9. Marx and Marx, *Lettres d'amour et de combat*, 37–38.
10. Marx and Marx, *Lettres d'amour et de combat*.
11. Karl Marx and Friedrich Engels, *The Communist Manifesto*, trans. Samuel Moore (Workers Educational Association, 1848).
12. Peck, *Jeune Karl Marx*.
13. Jenny Marx-Longuet, "Escape from Paris," *Woodhull & Claflin's Weekly*, 21 October 1871. https://www.marxists.org/archive/marx/bio/family/jenny/1871-fr.htm.

14. Rachel Holmes, *Eleanor Marx: A Life* (Bloomsbury Press, 2014).
15. "Lizzie Burns," DBpedia, accessed November 28, 2024, https://dbpedia.org/page/Lizzie_Burns.
16. Holmes, *Eleanor Marx*.
17. Karl Marx, *Capital: A Critical Analysis of Capitalist Production,* trans. Samuel Moore and Edward Aveling (Swan Sonnenschien, 1887).
18. Holmes, *Eleanor Marx*.
19. Holmes, *Eleanor Marx,* xii.
20. Holmes, *Eleanor Marx*, 3.
21. Eleanor Marx speaking at Aurora Turner Hall in Chicago, November 8, 1886, as part of a fifteen week speaking tour with Edward Aveling. Roberta Ferrari, "Not Just a Woman. The Agitation Tour in the US and the Proletariat Feminism of Eleanor Marx," *Journal of American History and Politics* 5 (2022): 49–59.
22. Edward Aveling and Eleanor Marx Aveling, *Labour Movement in America* (Forgotten Books, 2018).
23. Friedrich Engels, *The Origin of the Family, Private Property, and the State*, with a new introduction by Tristram Hunt (Penguin Classics, 2010).
24. Edward Aveling and Eleanor Marx Aveling, "The Woman Question," *Westminster Review* 125 (January 1886): 207–22.
25. Marx, *Capital*.
26. Hendrik Ibsen, *A Doll's House and Two Other Plays*, trans. R.F. Sharp and Eleanor Marx Aveling (Dent, 1910).
27. Gustav Flaubert, *Madame Bovary,* trans. Eleanor Marx Aveling, with a new introduction by Ferdinand Brunetiere (Neeland Media, 2015).
28. Holmes, *Eleanor Marx*.
29. Chicago, *Dinner Party*.

30. Edward Aveling and Eleanor Marx-Aveling, "More Socialist Personalities: The Women Delegates at the International Congress," *Westminster Gazette*, August 19, 1893.
31. Alexandra Kollontai, "Communism and the Family," in *Selected Writings of Alexandra Kollontai*, trans. A. Holt (Allison & Busby, 1977).

**Valérie Lefebvre-Faucher** is editor-in-chief of *Liberté: Art and Politics* magazine. She has worked as an editor at both Remue-ménage and Écosociété, with a focus on environmental, anti-capitalist, and feminist work. In addition to having collaborated with numerous collectives, blogs, and magazines, she co-edited the book *Faire Partie du Monde* and published *Procès Verbal*. She lives in Montreal, Quebec.

**Mélissa Bull** is a writer, editor, and translator based in Montreal. She has published a collection of poetry, *Rue*, a collection of short stories, *The Knockoff Eclipse*, and has translated such works as Nelly Arcan's collection *Burqa of Skin* and Marie-Sissi Labrèche's novel *Borderline*. Her translation of Maxime Raymond Bock's novel, *Morel*, was a finalist for the 2024 Governor General's Award.